Surviving

Kearsen Avendano

Surviving copyright © 2023 by Kearsen Avendano

All rights reserved. No part of this book may be reproduced or transmitted in any form or by any means- electronic, mechanical, photocopy, recording, or any other- except for brief quotations in printed reviews, without the prior permission of the publisher.

ISBN: 979-8-9894457-0-7

Published in the United States by Avendano Books.

First Edition 2023

Kearsenavendano.com

Important Note From The Author

We've all been through pain and darkness at some point. But you don't have to hide it; your pain isn't any less important than another's. Your pain matters.

This book is my letter to *you*.

This book is to help you feel seen, heard, and understood. I want you to know that you are not alone or stuck. These pages hold the truth, the voice that you need to hear above every other.

As you go through, be kind to yourself. Be patient with yourself. Take care of yourself. Feel every emotion, let it break through your walls. Let it stream down the river and burst into the clouds. Let it out.

There will be biblical affirmations at the back of this book. Please don't be afraid to use it, take a break, or ask for help.

The first section of this book is called The Darkest Valley. In this section, you will find pieces that contain the feelings one may have as they struggle through the darkness. They also include themes mentioned under the "Trigger Warning" note.

The second section is Between The Waters. This part was created for when you are starting to have hope but are still fighting to make it out of the pain. It represents the back and forth of the waves that crash against us when we are so close to escaping, yet it still feels far.

The final section is Light Of Life. Here, you will find the light in its fullness and something to hold onto. This part is where great strength and hope are waiting for you

Read whatever you need to, whenever you need it.

And remember to take it one page at a time.

Trigger Warning

The poem below lists the themes that this book contains.

Loneliness tangles itself to become one with depression, often leaning on anxiety, creating a storm that welcomes insecurity, tempting self-harm, and beckoning for negative and suicidal thoughts.

The shadows whisper fears of repeated abandonment, infidelity, and abuse. Sexual, emotional, and even physical. It pushes you to reach out to the substances, to take another step further into the dark.

It won't. Because even though you may be blind to it now, a ray peeks through the clouds, tearing every wall down, the mere touch bringing them to ashes. It sparks hope inside, igniting a fire of strength, spreading faith to every corner, and leaving victory in its wake. Because time and time, we see that in the light, every shadow flees. And from the ashes, a new creation breathes.

For extra caution, each negative theme is also listed below:
>
> Loneliness
> Depression
> Anxiety
> Negative Thoughts

Abandonment
Insecurity
Self-Harm
Suicidal Ideations
Sexual Abuse
Physical Abuse
Emotional Abuse
Infidelity
Substance Abuse

Dedication

To my husband,
I've seen your silent pain, how your mind unravels in the middle of the day. Watching your features fight to be still, to hide the chaos running wild inside.
I've seen the smile, afraid to arise, unknown to the day or even the world. A pure smile, finally being born, spreading its wings and ready to soar.

To you,
The one whose eyes read the words that line each page. Waiting to be seen, to be heard. Wanting, just for once, to not be alone in the world. In need of hope, even the smallest grain. In need of a light, in need of some strength.

Contents

THE DARKEST VALLEY 11

IN BETWEEN THE WATERS 47

LIGHT OF LIFE 111

THE DARKEST VALLEY

Kearsen Avendano

My ribs were feathers
Protecting my soft heart
You came crashing in
Breaking me entirely with every word
One by one destroying me
You never stopped until my heart did
That night I died
You finally realized just how fragile I was

Surviving

They never loved you
They just wanted to see how long it would take
To break you
Words only ever holding emptiness
As their hands deliver the colored splotches
To your delicate skin

They never loved you
They just wanted to lay claim
To own you
Steadily increasing the control
Tightening their hold
Chaining you down
Never to let go

Kearsen Avendano

Chasing after this image
Just a part to play
Drawing the smile to mimic
And avoid the words I struggle to say

Another face
On the body of a broken soul
Aching to fit in with the world
Tightening the strings to appear whole

Surviving

Gravel punctures my feet
Leaving behind dirt on the soles
Heart beating through my chest
Steadily pushing faster, harder
Quickened gasps escaping my lips

Rushing out

Then in

Hoping to keep pace with the beats
Fear coursing into my thoughts
Surrounding my sight
Pulling me down
Further from the light

Kearsen Avendano

Silence does not always bring peace. Sometimes, it's in the silence that you break completely. You stumble, trying to carry the pieces and hold them in place. But in the silence, they seem to slip through your fingers, falling to the ground to shatter once more, increasing the number of cracks along your soul.

Surviving

We are not okay
But people don't understand that
They don't understand

So we sit here
Apologizing for things
As if they are the ones going through the pain
We apologize for the broken hearts
Lonely tears
Red marks
Little pills
The lost years

They call us selfish
Crazy
Foolish
For a sickness that tears us apart limb by limb
And cell by cell
A sickness that has us up late nights
Aching for help
Just to keep repeating itself
Day in
And day out
A never ending cycle of
Standing on the edge of wanting to be okay
But knowing you're not

So they tell us we have a choice
Yet we are letting this happen
As if we can control it?
No, it controls us
We spend months
Years

Kearsen Avendano

Trying to grip the handles and change the gears
Each time we do
Getting thrown deeper back into it

As if we are lost at sea
Coming across a shore
Hoping it holds safety
Though the things on land drive us crazy
Making us dive further into the water

Then we drown
Knowing that if to ask for help
We somehow become the criminal
Instead of the victim
We aren't what it shows
We are better people
Stuck behind a wall built of pain and suffering

And if you're lucky to find a crack
To be set free
Run and never return
Never again meet the sea

Surviving

Slowly I lost them all
Every person in my life
Until I was only left with you
Captured in your grasp
Hanging on to every word you spoke
Ready to meet your request
Your love being my hope
A love so suffocating
That I never noticed
Until the breath left my lungs
At the flick of your wrist

Kearsen Avendano

Whispers falling from your tongue
Quiet
And deadly
Boots disappearing from the door frame
Leaving drawers of empty promises
And broken dreams
Wasted time
Silent screams
Pieces of a future
That'll never be reached

Surviving

I can feel the pain
I guess that's something right
Better than not feeling anything
Except I'd rather not feel
I'd rather not wish for a hundred endings
Or for the world to cave in on itself
I'd rather not feel the damage inflicted upon my heart
Upon my skin
Burrowing deep into my mind
Controlling every thought
I would give these feelings up to become numb
To be free from the dread that cages me
Using my torment as it's entertainment
Hollowed out
Drained of life
I'd rather not feel at all

        …if that is alright

Kearsen Avendano

They said it was a mistake
It was out of their hands
They couldn't lose you
Just one more chance

If it were a mistake
Why'd it happen again

Surviving

Not knowing the truth, the answers to every question that runs across your mind will only create a storm of emotions. Tangled together, stuck between hoping and dying at the same time. So, you replay every good thing until the bad falls through the memories, and you realize that maybe it really wasn't meant to be.

Kearsen Avendano

It's because of me
Isn't it

I'm the reason for your every anger
The way your words spit at my face
Hands threatening to leave their mark
I tried to be careful
Watch what I say
But it's never enough

In your eyes
It'll always be my fault

Surviving

All you wanted was for them to notice you
Everything you did for them
All the love you poured out
Every line crossed
How you tore the walls down
You just wanted them to see you
Because every night
Their body laid in bed with yours
While their mind
Was nowhere in sight

Kearsen Avendano

I don't speak of the pain I feel inside. Because how do I tell you that sometimes I want to die, feeling this sorrow deep in my soul? The fear that breaks from the shadows, the one that says that I'll never be whole. How would you understand it when you can't simply place a bandage?

Surviving

You pulled me in
Becoming the comfort I didn't know I needed
Filling my arms with the gifts of your love
My mind with your words of assurance
You were my knight in shining armor
I just didn't realize I was the one in need of armor
Because it wasn't long before you became something else entirely
A monster
Leaving my mind in shambles
As my body would tremble at the thought of you
Steadying my balance
To walk the shells in your presence

Now that you're gone
I'm left to react to every person the same
Always on alert
Afraid to hear your name
Or see your face
Aching to feel just a glimpse of peace
Aching to truly escape

Kearsen Avendano

The smell of roses fills my nose
Petals cascading around me
Blending into the puddle at my feet
Hidden away from every cruelty
Swallowed by my touch
For everything I love falls to pieces
Simply following my own heart's lead
This darkness so quiet and lonely
I stay waiting for relief

Surviving

I tear the clothes off my skin to keep your wounds at bay, doing all that I can to try and make you stay. Pouring from an empty cup, I filled yours to the brim. I love you; you are my world, so you'd say again. I opened myself up to you and ignored every fear. And every time, you promised me you wouldn't leave me here. Until one night, I woke to you doing as every other does. Planning to abandon me in the dark of night, proving there was never any love.

Kearsen Avendano

I keep replaying it
Every thing I did
Or didn't do
All the words that hung on my lips
But never rolled off my tongue
How I could've been better for you
I lay here
Cold and alone
Reliving every moment that went wrong
And sometimes I let the thoughts run
The ones that wonder if you relive it too

Surviving

Tell me.
Was it worth it in the end,
Choosing those drugs over me again?

Kearsen Avendano

Thoughts dance along the edge of my mind, waiting to pounce into the depths. They run wild with no way to leash them, to reel them in again. Quickly, they combine before splitting and multiplying. Further and further into the hole, digging and digging until I can't see the top anymore. Steadily, each word circles me on repeat, keeping hold of my mind, engraving its hands into my feet.

Surviving

I lost myself to meet your every desire
Chipping away pieces of who I was
Trying to become a perfect sculpture
Free of any flaws
But I never could
No matter how much I broke off
The flaws ran too deep
Still
I continued to carve
Until I was nothing but rubble
Used beneath your feet

Kearsen Avendano

I loved you
Even after you broke me
I loved you
Even after you bruised me
Tore me apart with your teeth
And stole the air so I couldn't breathe
I still loved you
But
You never once loved me

Surviving

Dreams turning to nightmares
A glimpse of the inevitable future
Where you don't return
And once again
I'm left all alone
Another lesson to learn

Kearsen Avendano

Sometimes I lie awake at night
After every body has fallen into slumber
I stare at the ceiling
Feeling a thousand feelings
All while feeling numb
I lay still
Barely breathing on the inside
Listening to every piece of my being break
Repeatedly shattering one by one
Sometimes I lie awake at night
And feel myself dying
But that's alright

Surviving

Old chapters play in my mind
At the most inconvenient of times
If only I could read them
Watch them
Without hating this thing called life

Kearsen Avendano

The waves washed over me
Drops clinging to my skin
Holding for dear life onto the body of another
Would they leave if they knew what they touched
There's darkness peeking through the cracks
Breathlessly singing to the drops
Drawing them near
If they could see
Would they run to the ground
Away from the depth that called out to them
That caressed their souls only to crush them
Would they have been better off letting go

Surviving

There are days where I can't feel. My mind goes blank, zoning out on the simplest of things. My heart feels dull, almost empty, almost like it's without a soul. Some days, I forget how to move or think. I stop fighting to survive, and I stay, waiting. Barely even being. Barely even breathing.

Kearsen Avendano

Shivers rack along my skin, slowly falling to the floor. My heart becomes numb as they close the door. Tears create a flood upon my face, drowning out the screams my lungs fail to make. Thoughts fight to form among the dread filling my bones, inching its way to the surface, destroying all that it touches. It shatters every breath I try to breathe, curled in the dark, finding the pain to be the only thing that comforts me. Even then, the pieces descend, sprawled out at my feet, as I struggle to put them back in. Jagged edges collide again, desperate to conceal the cracks in between, though I know deep down that I will never be the same. After all, when this happens, there is always a piece unable to be saved.

Broken beyond measure, it will always remain.

Surviving

Chains rattle against my skin
Echoing from my soul
Screaming at my mind
Thoughts demanding control
Grasping to take hold
Of my entire being
Desperate to be my world
The only thing I ever see

Blinding my eyes
Stealing my life
Filling my head
With horrid lies
Wanting to consume
Every part of me
Until nothing is left
But a shell that is empty

Taking over my surroundings
Silencing my cries
So that no one can hear me
But the darkness inside
Words crushing my heart
Breaking the will I had to live
Slowly driving me insane
My only comfort
My only friend

My every pain

Kearsen Avendano

How am I supposed to move on,
To heal from one abuse,
When I still suffer from another?

Surviving

I see the forced smiles that you fill your days with. Every laugh pushed out, hoping to fit. I see the lonely moments through your days when the thoughts decide they won't keep at bay. I see how your body sinks under the weight. Feet slipping, legs buckling. Hardly able to move, feeling as though you're already gone. Lost to the emptiness, waiting for the night so you can drift into the abyss. Praying to at least find sleep, again, each day on repeat, you lay stuck in this cycle of quiet heaviness. I see how you constantly hope for just a minute, a second, of rest.

Kearsen Avendano

Surviving

IN BETWEEN THE WATERS

Surviving

Kearsen Avendano

Some of us have always been broken inside. Pieces shoved together to fit the mold that we are whole. We fill the shoes you provide, hoping to be all you wish for.

But you don't see it's not about being fixed or whole. It's the hope to be made new, to be what we haven't been before. Not going back to what you wanted us to be, but looking to what the future holds, looking forward to the more.

Surviving

I know you're scared to have hope or even the smallest of joy, feeling as though the second you do, it'll get ripped away. I know how terrifying it is to think of no longer being bound by it: the darkness, the pain, the hurt.

But I promise you, you can. You will. If you open up to me, hold on to me. Let me help you become free.

Kearsen Avendano

Your pain matters
It deserves to be heard
To be seen
Every piece of you
Do not be ashamed

Surviving

Stop listening to the lies that plague your mind.
You were always enough,
From your very first cry.

Kearsen Avendano

You may have fallen, but you have not failed. Even if you give up, I will be here to lift you back up. To guide the way and light the path for your feet to follow.

In every way you go,
I will have gone before.
Shielding and protecting you,
Forevermore.

Surviving

You set impossible standards for yourself
Lifting the bar each time
Pushing for the perfect outcome
Racing to cross that line

Taking the weight upon your shoulders
No matter how much
Afraid to ask for help
Believing that if you fail
You simply aren't enough

It's okay to need someone
To reach out for a hand
It's okay to let things drop
To not be able to stand
It doesn't define your worth
Or the strength you hold within

You are worthy
You are strong
You are brave
You are enough

You always have been

Kearsen Avendano

Tell me again
Of your love and devotion
Sing them to me
So I can play it on repeat

                              Tell me again
                        How you'll never leave
                      Let it soak into my heart
                      So I may finally believe

Tell me again
That I may be at peace
Forgetting of the ones
That abandoned me

                              Tell me again
                          Tell me once more
                          Tell me forever
                          Tell me you're sure

Surviving

My love is endless.

                Don't be scared,

                                To get lost in it.

Kearsen Avendano

Shadows running, eager to escape. Crawling into crevices, hiding within your body as the light breaks through. The light fills every inch of the room before slowly filling you, burning the darkness from within, destroying that which surrounds. Bringing life into your eyes, placing your feet on solid ground. Wiping every fear from the depths of your mind, replacing it with hope. A hope that, till now, was only ever pined.

Surviving

Wounds take time
To become scars
It needs healing
Which can be hard
Don't be afraid
Of what it takes
Just slow down
And have some faith
Take one step
And you will see
I'm right here
It's you and me

Kearsen Avendano

You fought to get to where you are
Don't let them pull you back
They never loved you
They only want to see you fall
While they stand over and laugh

Surviving

Don't listen to their voices
The words spewed from their mouths
They will fade
And wither away
While you grow and rise
In strength

Kearsen Avendano

Their words mean nothing,
When their hands break you entirely.

Surviving

You are not the lies they speak
Or what they try to do
It is not your fault
It doesn't fall on you
They don't want you to see
The worth that you carry
They don't want you to know
Of your true identity

Kearsen Avendano

Things may not be perfect
You may feel stuck
Trapped in the current
Constantly trying to escape
From a never ending maze
Unsure of where to go
Feeling lost in the midst
The walls climbing higher
With every glance

Don't let it deceive
Or blind you with fear
They aren't as tall
As they appear
Those walls can be broken
Brought to the ground
Falling before you
Crumbling down

Surviving

I know it hurts
And feels unfair
But I promise there's more
Than you're aware
Everything you could ever dream
And more than you can think
A fully different life
A beautiful reality

Kearsen Avendano

I see your exhaustion, every thought, and anxiety that consumes your mind. The numbness inching upon your heart.

But,

I'll be your shield, your every piece of armor. When you don't have the strength to stand, let alone fight, I will be by your side. Through every day and every night. Whenever you become terrified, I am there for you. I will hold you when the waters flood. When all your hopes run dry, when you can't see the light.

And I will remind you that you're not your mistakes; you are not your pain. Please, look at me. Don't hide your face. Don't be ashamed of the parts that ache. I won't ever walk away.

I choose you a million times.

Surviving

Your feelings are real
Every single one
Even the scary ones
Don't be afraid
To let them out
Don't be afraid
To break

It's in the breaking
That you have strength
In the feeling
And letting go
That you can be remade

Kearsen Avendano

You're supposed to love
Hate
Hurt
Break

You're supposed to let it out
Because no matter the pain
You're going to be okay
You're going to survive this

Surviving

It's okay to feel, to cry even. It's not a weakness but a strength. Strength to feel the pain, to get through that pain. To get through each day and come out the other side of it.

You are not weak; you are brave.

Kearsen Avendano

You have to feel everything
All the grief
The loss
And pain
Managing it
Controlling it
Only gives it control over you
So release all you've shoved down
Let it burst out

Surviving

There is more to me
Than you give me credit for
I am enough
I deserve to be loved as such
And I will no longer accept anything less
Nor will I fall under your touch
The tight grip of your fist
Will not be my guide
And you
Will no longer be missed
For I have finally opened my eyes

Kearsen Avendano

I've been with you through every dark valley that blinded your eyes, even the ones that ripped the colors from your sight. It left you to stare in the mirror at what lies on the other side, always reaching out for them yet struggling to find.

But I see your true colors, even with the pain that you hold. I see the real you when all you see is the old. You won't find yourself when you reach for this world. But instead, when you stop listening to the lies that you're told.

Your worth and value are greater than you realize. Just because you don't see it doesn't mean it's not inside. You are more, you are beautiful. You can be whole; you can be bright.

I know it's hard; I know it hurts. But trust me and open your eyes.

Surviving

It's okay to be broken
To be depressed
It's okay to be exhausted
To be in pain
I will bring you the peace that you need
The quiet that you crave
And a comfort that will wash over you in waves

It's okay to cry
To scream
It's okay to crumble
To grieve
My arms are before you
Ready to hold your every piece
Ready to help you create a new thing

It's okay to smile
To believe
It's okay to laugh
To be free
I hold my hand to you
Waiting for you to take it
And reach all that you can be

You're not alone
You may not see me
But I'm by your side
I'm holding your hand
Holding your heart
And I'll hold all you can't carry
I'll hold every part

Kearsen Avendano

Stop overthinking and letting the thoughts lead you down that winding road. It'll only take you to a dead-end tunnel. Instead, hand them to me. And in return, I'll bring you peace.

    A silence

        A stillness

                Whatever you need, it will be.

Surviving

They may have left you broken and bruised. One after another, ghosts disappearing behind the door. Each taking a small piece of who you were, chained to their hands, dragging along the floor. The fleeting moments that play inside your mind, wishing to grasp onto the good while your heart continues to crack. Fingers searching for a comfort that has left you behind, terrified.

You may have felt so empty and alone, brought to your knees as the pain soars, unable to think or breathe. Unable to see anything beyond what lay in front of your feet. Beyond the tears that drowned your cries and filled your ears.

They may have left you, but I never have.

I sat with you as your body felt it could give no more. My arms held you when your cries were but whispers and when the sound rose higher than ever before. My cries echoed your own, and my heart felt for the hurt you endured. My comfort surrounded you, lifted you on the days you barely held on and the nights you let go.

I have been by your side, lifting and carrying you, pouring into you. I have never left, and I never will. Even when you can stand, I will continue to hold your hand.

Kearsen Avendano

Stop focusing on what you see
What's in front of your eyes
You will come out
You will rise
And in that
You'll say goodbye
To what was before
To all you survived

Surviving

Have you seen yourself trapped inside your mind? Curled into the corner, full of chains anchored to the walls, darkness consuming every inch. Shivering, almost numb. Face hidden away, scared to entertain any hope. Feeling as though an empty shell is all there will ever be.

Have you seen healing? Chains crumbling to the ground, turning to ashes. Eyes igniting like a match, hope burning deep inside. Its flames spread, bringing light to the room, taking down every wall, bringing life to that shell as you break free and take back control.

Kearsen Avendano

Let their boots walk away from you
Never to return
I know the pain will come
And the loneliness hurts
But they'll never again
Steal the air from your lungs
And when the sorrow comes
Remember
There is comfort in my arms

Surviving

You may see yourself in pieces, bits, and shards, torn apart by the pain. But I see you as clay, able to be made new. Able to grow, to heal.

So leave the pieces on the floor; they are old and broken. It's time to create, not reuse. Don't get stuck trying to hold them together, allowing them to slice into your skin, causing a steady flow of control and the hurt and reminder that you were not whole.

You are not that same person. Let the pieces go. Stop holding on to the dark, to the lies it spoke. It is not your friend but instead your foe. The pressure you felt was not comfort but its grasp around your soul. Now, it can reach you no more.

Kearsen Avendano

Don't let the doubt invade your thoughts. The lies it whispers are no more than dust. No matter what comes against you, I am for you; I will remain.

I will never leave you; I will stay and love you just the same.

Surviving

I know you think you have nothing to give
Left at rock bottom by every person before
Barely enough energy to lift your head from the floor
I know that you're scared
Refusing to believe it
Lift your eyes to look beyond
And truly see it

To see the next step
Instead of the risk
It will be the first
Out of the abyss

Kearsen Avendano

Stop collecting every emotion in the furthest parts of yourself, burying it down, waiting for every strand to disappear from your eyes. Even though you remove it from sight, it still lives deep inside, building up more and more pressure each time. Until it becomes too much, exploding within, causing the pain to escape and wreak havoc on your body, bringing about every emotion once again.

Smash your inner bottle, and let the screams break out from your lungs. Let the anger erupt from your fists. Feel something, feel anything.

Feel everything.

Let it flood until it doesn't exist. Because to feel is not weak, but instead a great strength. That's when healing can begin, hope can enter, and faith can sprout from the depths, growing to achieve your dreams that before had been crushed. No longer merely silhouettes, but now able to be touched.

Surviving

You won't find help at the bottom of a bottle, only a truth that's hard for you to swallow. A number on your days that's steadily decreasing. And your body still in pain, one that's only increasing.

If you want help, then lay it all down. Feel your pain and let it out. Don't become the bottle you downed by burying it inside. Give peace to your mind. Peace to your heart and peace to your soul. Let it go, hear my words, and believe in me so you can heal.

Kearsen Avendano

You don't have to speak the words because I hear your heart, the aching it endures. I see your eyes and the pain they hide, the exhaustion that wraps around your body and mind. The shiver of fear that runs along every promise that there's better. You don't have to speak for me to know because

    I *see*

    I *hear*

    I *care*

I will comfort you through every moment and every tear. I will remind you that love eliminates fear. And I'll continue to give you hope in what's to come. I'll give you strength to continue to go on.

Surviving

Let every stone fall from around your heart
Allow me to chip away the walls that trap you
The ones that leave you cold and alone
Stuck in an empty darkness

One by one
Each piece will fall
And my voice will break through
Reaching you
Touching your heart
Bringing a light and warmth you never knew
Sparking a hope inside your soul
That I will guide you to
And instead of cement
You will be planted
Able to grow into something new

Kearsen Avendano

Don't forgive them for their sake. Forgive them for yours. Holding on to it only creates more pain in your soul, making you relive the moment over again and delaying you from moving on.

Forgiveness is not to forget. It's not to let go of the memory but instead to let go of the emotions it brings. The ones that leave you feeling empty.

To do this is not to welcome them back with open arms. But to take separate paths and avoid further harm. The goal is not to put them at ease, only to bring you peace. To help you be free.

Free of the anger, free of the pain. Free from having it burden you. Freedom from the chains.

Surviving

Forgive yourself for what you couldn't do
Even for what you did
Forgive yourself for the words you spoke
And for the ones that you hid

                    Forgive yourself for staying too long
                    For not believing what you were told
                    Forgive yourself for the things of the past
                    You are no longer of the old

You are now a new creation
Made from a different mold
And this you deserves forgiveness
Deserves to be whole

                    It's time to wipe the slate clean
                    And take back what the pain stole
                    To heal yourself completely
                    Mind, body, spirit, and soul

Kearsen Avendano

Having hope is hard. Stepping out of the pain, away from the dark, is hard. Breaking the chains from your body, the ones that controlled your mind is hard.

It's scary to hope for better when you've never had it. When all you've known is the opposite. It's scary to be vulnerable in that hope. To let yourself want it and dream of it.

But, just because it hasn't happened yet, doesn't mean it won't. Don't let the fear talk you out of reaching it. Don't let the chains keep you from receiving it.

Hope is beautiful and filled with happiness, filled with love, and a better life. Hope is of what is to come. In hope you're not alone. Lean on the strength of the light and let it guide you in hope. Let it guide you to a safe home. A home where you are free. Free and finally happy.

Surviving

It's there in the midst of all the pain. It's there as you stand in the middle of the darkness. When everything seems impossible, and your surroundings begin to crumble.

There, as you're falling to your knees, begging for someone, for anyone to see. As the world spins and you're left,

wondering,
hoping,
praying.

That's when miracles happen. That's when the seemingly impossible unravels to show the way. To show the possible, to provide for your escape.

Kearsen Avendano

I've seen you fight when you were completely exhausted. I've seen you pick yourself up when you were broken. I've seen the tears and the screams, every day you felt alone, and the nights you lost hope.

I've seen you hide behind a smile. Pretending to be something you're not, just to get by. Afraid of being a burden and suffering in silence. I've seen each time you were strong for others even though inside you were dying.

I've seen you hope for something better, letting the dreams fill your mind. Grasping onto them for just a moment of relief, of escape from your current life.

I've seen you pray; I've seen you wish; I've seen you beg with all your might. For peace and love, for a chance to be in the light.

I've seen you for who you are. Not what you display. I've seen you for who you'll be once you finally escape.

Surviving

You may not see the way right now,
                trust me, and you will.

You may not see the better from where you are,
                believe in me still.

Know that I am always guiding you, creating the path for your feet to follow. My light will bring life to fill every part of you that's hollow.

Kearsen Avendano

Someone once told me that when darkness enters your soul, it's always a piece of you. But that's not true because when you're made new, the old pieces are no more. The broken and bruised edges drift to the bottom of the ocean. They burn to ash, crumbling, ceasing to exist, floating away in the wind.

So, if you have a piece that contains darkness, don't worry or be afraid. It will be removed, no longer having control over you.

No longer being a part of you.

Surviving

How do I love you
When I can barely look in the mirror
Plagued by their voice on repeat in my head
Reminding me of every flaw
Telling me I'm not enough
That everything I am
Everything I do is wrong

How do I love you
When my thoughts taunt me
Creating problems that don't exist
Spreading lies at my feet
Whispering of our demise
And the pain that'll come
Replaying every fear
That for you I'm not the one

Kearsen Avendano

How do you love me
By just being you
Speaking every worry
Every pain
Every truth

Tell me
So I can reassure of my love
Tell me
Let me hold every cry that you sob
Tell me
And I'll replace all those lies with what's true
Tell me
Allow me
To truly love you

Surviving

Show me your worst, the darkness that leaped inside your soul, digging into your heart as it breaks everything in sight.

Show me your pain. The one that leaves you screaming into the silence before abandoning a numb body in the emptiness.

Show me the pieces that tear you apart, the shame that has taken control, the guilt that racks your body whole.

Show me so that I can show you.

I will show you love for your worst, lifting your head and spreading light through you, reminding you of your true worth.

I will show you healing for your pain, helping your heart find forgiveness and peace, freeing your body from every chain.

I will show you comfort for each shattered piece, engulfing you in my arms, removing every shame that called your name. Helping you to let go of the brokenness and find a new strength.

Kearsen Avendano

Look past the trauma that blurs your vision. I know it's left a mark on your soul and in your mind.

I'm not telling you to forget it.
I'm saying to forgive it.

Surviving

Fear is not your future
Heartbreak is not your home
Step out of this pit
Break the chains off your arms
Don't be afraid
This is not who you are

You are more than the shame
Than the guilt
And the scars
There is more for you
Than the suffering
In your heart

Kearsen Avendano

Don't let the doubt sink into your skin, nibbling on your hope, eating away at your faith.

Look at me, hear my voice. I have told you what is to come. I have told you it will get better. The plans you've been given are only the start of what I have for you. The dreams that you hold onto are one of many that you will see.

Listen to what I speak. Don't look at what surrounds you because it is only temporary. Keep your eyes on me, take my hand, and believe in me.

Surviving

Sitting upon a tightrope
Feeling the wind blow
Dancing upon your skin
Stuck holding on for life
Scared to loosen your grip
Not knowing which way to go
What to think
Or what to hope
Unable to trust yourself
Unable to move an inch

Looking at the distance
Not knowing what lies below
So afraid of the unknown
You continue to hold on to the rope
But as it burns into your hands
A voice breaks through

Whispering

Breathing

Into you

"Trust in me
Have faith in what I speak
Allow me to hold you
Let go and believe"

Kearsen Avendano

Don't let the sorrow fill your smile
I know it can be hard to let it go
But remember that you are not this person anymore

You are not your past
Or the tears that drown your heart
You are not the trauma
That grips you for dear life
You are not the pieces
Shattered at your feet
Covered in tape and glue
Wanting so badly to be whole again
When in reality
You have to be made new

So open your eyes
It's time to go
Sometimes we must say goodbye
In order to say hello

Surviving

Look past the trauma
Come out of the shame
See the worth
That's on your name
A worth so great
So priceless
And new

Open your eyes to finally see *you*

Don't be afraid of becoming them. There hasn't been a time that you've even been close to it. You have always been the opposite. Not only contradicting who they are but what they said you'd be. You've broken every chain that was on you; overcome all that came against you. You've survived the pain that once consumed.

Their story is not your reality.

Surviving

If you can't believe there is better, then trust in me. If you can't hold on to hope or see anything other than the pain, hold on to me. If you can't see anything, listen to me.

I am here for you every step of the way. Through the valley and the depths of the sea, whatever it takes to get you to see and reach.

Trust in me.

Kearsen Avendano

When you're crushed
I will build you up
When you've fallen
I will remind you I'm all in
When you're broken
You'll see my arms are open

And when your heart has turned to pieces
You'll find that seed
The one that contains who you'll be
Once you're healed
Once you're whole
Once you're freed

Surviving

Tear down every wall that surrounds
Remove the mask from your face
Show who you truly are
Reveal your hurt
Your truth
And shame
Reveal your worth
Your beauty
And strength

Lay down the pieces
Let go of the tape
It's time to leave behind the bruises
To permanently escape
No longer briefly in the dreams of each day
But forever far from this pain

Stand up
Breathe
Don't listen to the fear
But focus on me
Don't look at the unknown
But look to those dreams

Remember the joy you hoped for
The change you begged for
The love you longed for
The peace you cried for
The healing you hesitated to believe
Each now within reach

Kearsen Avendano

Because
Once you can see past that darkness
Your eyes open to these promises
Your hands touch them
Your heart receives
All these things
Can now finally be

Surviving

Your pain was not meaningless
Every part of it matters
You can heal from it
You can use it
You can make a difference
Even if right now
It doesn't make sense

Kearsen Avendano

It can be scary
Not knowing what to do
Or where to go
Not having anyone or anything to turn to
Feeling alone

It can be scary
To want and hope
So badly for better
But not see it in front of you
To try and trust so much
For so long
While your surroundings continue to crumble

It can be scary
To not know what lies ahead
To look out at that next step
And see the cliffs edge

It can be scary
But I am guiding you along the way
I have promised you these things
And I stay true to what I say

Surviving

I hear your cries just as I hear your silence. I feel the breaking of your heart and the numbness that begins to crawl. I see the dullness that overtakes your eyes and the hurt that steals your smile.

I'm here with you through it all. No matter the pain, I'm not leaving you. No matter what it takes, I will help you through. Even in the darkness,

I love you.

Kearsen Avendano

Surviving

LIGHT OF LIFE

Surviving

Kearsen Avendano

I know you're scared to hope. To want so much for something better when nothing has gotten better. It hurts to believe for more as you struggle to get through even a minute of the day.

I know, but…

Believe anyway.
Hope, anyway.

Because it'll hurt whether you do or not, but with this, at least there will be minutes where you will escape the pain. Or even just seconds of a place you can go in your mind, in your heart. A place to feel the love, warmth, joy, and peace you wish for. At least, there will be something to hold on to. Something that gives you just a little more strength, a little more fight to make it another day.

And when you get there, when you make it to that place where you no longer have to imagine and escape, you'll feel it not just for a brief moment or a day but for eternity. You'll reach the better that was held in those glimpses of hope, in the dreams that you were so terrified to have. And you'll be thankful that you had them, that you took the risk.

Because no matter how far it seemed to be or how dark the world became. You chose to believe. And in turn, you overcame.

Surviving

They were wrong,
Love does overcome all.
It already has.
And if you let it,
You'll see that it truly is enough.

Kearsen Avendano

I loved you then
I'll love you now

Set down your fight
Give me your heart
Place your hand in mine
Step out of the dark
And into the light

All the lies
Will turn to ash
Every trauma
Of the past
The fear
The guilt
The sorrow
The shame

All of this
I will break

Surviving

You may not see it or see me. But hear me when I say there is a way out of this, a way through this. It won't always be easy; it won't always be pretty. But I can promise it's worth it. I can promise there's peace when you come out of it. A joy that you've never seen, filling you with a love and comfort unlike any other.

You may not believe the words that I speak. But trust me when I tell you that you'll find shelter with me, a safe place where you can feel comfortable and unashamed. You can lift your head; you can open your eyes and begin to see a glimpse of the light. You can see what it is to live and not just be alive.

Kearsen Avendano

Give me your hope
Give me your faith
Let me
Show you the way

Surviving

You are worthy of love
No matter where you came from
Or who you came from

You are worthy of love
Just as you are
And where you are

You are worthy of love
Not for who you were before
But for who you've become

You are worthy of love
The same love you pour into others
The love that for yourself you're still learning to harbor

Kearsen Avendano

Stop running from me
Hiding away from my eyes
Scared as to what I would find
Who I would find
You are worthy of saving
No matter how broken you may feel
Or how far gone you believe you are

Give me your hand
One breath at a time
One foot in front of the other
We will make our way to the light
Together

Surviving

I see you reaching for more
Craving for things to change
For the better to come
To be free from the pain

Don't give up
You'll see it soon
Just a little further
A little longer
You're almost there
I promise you

Kearsen Avendano

I will tell you over again.
Where you go, I will be. Where you lay your head, I will
watch over. Every step that you take, I will lead the way.
Every tumble that may come, I will lift you again.

Though the waters may get rough, I will be with you.
When the rivers become too much, I will help you
through. When the fire gets too hot, I will protect you.
And when the flames dance around, know that with me,
there is always a way out.

Through every valley,
across every desert,
under every sea.
I will always be,
with you.

Surviving

Let the wind wrap around you
Embracing you with my arms
Filling you with a new breath
Showing you what's to come

Allow the light to shine in
Breaking through the dark
Healing all that's within
Opening your eyes
Bringing a new vision

Kearsen Avendano

Lay it down
Every fear
Every doubt
Lay it down
Every burden
Every mountain

Break up the ground
Remove the roots that burrow
Deep into the pain
Say goodbye to the past
And to any shame

Lay it down
Every lie
Every frown
Lay it down
Every tear
Every drought

Make room for the new
For who you can be
For a new life
Where you will finally
Be free

Surviving

You are a seed
Sunken in the soil
Breaking apart
Surrounded by the dark
Beginning to doubt

But if you wait
And believe
You'll then be able to see
The light that comes through
How it calls to you
Not to fix your pieces
But rather fix you
Not to mend the seed
But create something new

You had to break before you could grow
And each shattered piece
You had to let go
To become whole
To become new

You are a flower
Beautiful and true

Kearsen Avendano

Open your eyes to see the beauty that is and could be. See the life that awaits you on the horizon. It may seem far, but I promise you will reach it. I promise you will fly, finally free from every pain, from everything that has ever held you down.

You will come out of the valley. Whether swimming, climbing, walking, or being carried. You will come out of it, stepping into the light that led you through it all, engulfed in the arms of every hope and dream. Of every want and need.

You will make it. Just keep your eyes on me. Keep your hand in mine. Listen to my voice. Know that you are safe and you are almost there.

You're almost there. We're almost there.

Surviving

You are not them
You are not their words
You are your own self
You always were

Kearsen Avendano

I am here to help you
Holding my hand to you
Waiting for you

Take my hand in yours
Let me hold you in my arms
Carrying every piece
And every scar

I'll catch your every tear
Comfort every cry
Remove all your burdens
And the pain in your mind

Surviving

Listen to my voice
To my words
Your every cry
Has been heard
Your every tear
I've caught with my hand
And with my feet
You will stand

Kearsen Avendano

I see your sorrow and hurting
The ache for healing
And the fear of whether you can reach it
Of what it would take to reach it
The wishing for something better
While being wrapped in the chains of before
Wondering if you could even get there
Scared to hope for more

You can achieve it
It's possible to reach
To take that first step
To actually believe
Stretch out your hand
Place it in mine
Let go of the chains
Let your bones come alive

Surviving

You may not see me, but I see you. I've heard your cries. I've seen your pain. And I've been here through every fire. Don't give up. Though you can't see it, I do. I see the dreams ahead of you, the ones that become reality. The plans that are waiting for you in the right time. These plans are only the beginning of what is to come. Should you continue and choose to put your hands in mine.

Kearsen Avendano

Pull back the curtain
Remove the napkin
Wipe your face clean
Step into the light
See who you can be
Should you stop hiding
And let yourself just be

Surviving

You no longer have to be misunderstood
You don't have to hide away the pain
Or continue to feel shame
You're broken
And that's okay
It doesn't matter what they say
Sometimes
To heal properly
You have to break

Kearsen Avendano

I know it's a lot to ask you to believe when you can't see it. Or to ask you to trust when you've been broken and beaten. I know it's a lot to put what's left of your heart out on the table. It's hard to be open and vulnerable. Giving the last few pieces of yourself, the ones that lay bloodied in your hands. The last few that remain after all that's happened.

I know it's a lot to ask. But I will ask again. Give me all that's left. Give me all of you. I want the broken pieces of you because you're valuable. You're worthy. You're beautiful. You are so much more than what you see. There is so much more than what you see. Please, let me guide you. Let me lead.

It might not make sense. Not in the moment, that is. But when you get there, when the brighter side is reached. When you escape and can breathe. I promise you'll finally see. And you'll be glad that you believed.

Surviving

I may not know how deep the pain goes. And every pain I may not even know. But what I do know is that I'm here raising my sword. Spiritually and physically. I am fighting with you, and if you can't continue, I will take your place. I will fight for you as I guard and keep you safe.

Kearsen Avendano

I know the darkness threatens to surround you
Inching closer
Thick clouds shuffling to blind you
Look at me instead
Keep your eyes on mine
Take my hand
Feel my skin
Know that you are not alone in this
Stand up and walk with me
Let me carry you if you need
But please
Hold onto me

Surviving

I promise you, you're not alone. And I'll remind you every day. I'll tell you every minute, every second if that's what it takes.

I am close to you. I will comfort you when you feel lonely. I will love you when you feel broken. I will hold you when you are fallen. I will be here through the dark, through every valley. Through the waters that rise and the ones that seem scary.

Through it all, it is you that I carry.

Kearsen Avendano

If you want to be healed, you need new pieces to build.

If you want to be new, you must let go of the person you knew.

Surviving

I will be your safe place, where you can go to be a mess. You can break down and fall apart; you can scream and shout. Show me it all. All the light and all the dark, flowing out of you like a rushing stream, give it to me.

I love all of you. I want all of you. Everything. The deepest, darkest parts of your being. The most vulnerable parts that you keep. Show me the light of the child lost within, your beautiful innocence.

No matter what you've gone through, I see that child in you. In need of love, in need of hope, in need of a home.

I will be whatever you need.

Kearsen Avendano

Hope is hard
As is faith
Standing up
And having strength
It doesn't take much
To make a difference
Just a little touch
And an ear to listen

                Surviving

                                Falling

                      Surrendering

          Trusting

Loving

Does not make you weak
But brave enough to take that step
And believe

Kearsen Avendano

I see your smile,
Stretching across your face so widely. Holding the bellow of a laugh that erupts so loudly. Words gifting joy to those that surround.

I see your eyes,
Aching to reach the light that your smile portrays. Falling short of this facade you try to display. Bearing every pain you hold deep within.

I see you,
Not the mask you use to pretend. The you deep inside, far past the grin. Who needs help to make it through the darkness that keeps you pinned.

I see the person that can be made completely new. Washed clean, healed, and given a different view. One that's full of hope, full of love, and full of you.

Surviving

It's not having the perfect appearance that makes you worthy and beautiful.
It's what's found within you.

And no matter how far you go or how much time passes, you'll always be just as precious.
Just as priceless.

Kearsen Avendano

You're not walking this valley alone
You're not on your own
I'm telling you
That I am here
Listen to what I say
You don't need to fear

Everything will be okay

Surviving

Be kind to yourself,
Oftentimes, wounds take years to scar.

Kearsen Avendano

You are stronger for having gone through what you did. You are stronger for making it. Every tear, every scar, has led you to where you are. And now, it's time to decide where to go from here. To let go of all the old, let go of every fear. Choose to step into the better, to step into the more. Choose to focus on what is to come and open a new door.

A door that brings hope for a better life. One where you can live and not just strive to survive. Filled with change, filled with love. Filled with a whole self, brand new. Filled with everything that's been awaiting you.

Surviving

You deserve to find forgiveness in yourself and for yourself. Letting go of the pain of the past once and for all. Letting go of the blame you've held in your heart.

To feel love that blossoms and grows, an unconditional love that's intimate and pure. One that keeps giving and sees you for who you are, even when you can't. That always stays through everything.

To have peace and rest in your soul. A restoration and freedom that you've yet to know. To be released from every chain there ever was. The feeling of every burden removed, and the breath brought back to you.

To know joy deep within your heart, filled with happiness and content. Made of kindness and strength that lasts all your days.

To be full of hope, inside and out, knowing that there is good ahead, without a doubt. To believe and see that there is light beyond every cloud.

To be new, free from the past. Free from every pain that held on for so long. A new person, a new heart, a new whole.

You deserve it all.

Kearsen Avendano

I will lead you through it
Every step of the way
Listen to my voice
And the words that I say

I will get you to it
You will be okay

Surviving

You are not too much
You are enough
You are not trapped
Or alone
My light shines
Breaking through the stone
I will pull you out
Give you my love
Give you my all
Because you're worth more
Than you'll ever know

Kearsen Avendano

I know it may have buckled your knees, bringing you to pieces on the floor. I know it may have destroyed you down to your core, tearing you apart one layer at a time. I know it may have scared your heart and your mind. I know it may have caused you to crumble to the ground. But your story just might be what helps another stand instead of drown.

Surviving

You matter to me
Your life is of worth
You are enough
You are adored

Kearsen Avendano

Remove the cement from your throat
One crack at a time
One piece at a time
One word at a time
Free yourself from their control
Step out of their lies

Tell your truth
Let it be found
All that was covered
Let it breathe
Let it out

Surviving

The wind whispers
Of a hope and a dream
A victory
Unlike any you've seen

It waits for you to finally believe
Every promise
Every need
Every change
It'll bring

Kearsen Avendano

It's not time to give up; it's time to hold on. Where you are now is not the end of your story but the beginning. There is more for you; there is better for you.

Please, keep going.

Surviving

When you make it through the wilderness
Out of the valley
Escaping the abyss
I am still with you
I still love you
Remember this

Kearsen Avendano

Give me the scars you hold, the ones that line your skin, the ones etched in your soul. Lay every crack into my hands so that I may seal them, never to break again. I will fill them with love and strength, hope and faith. No longer broken pieces but pieces new and whole. Something that has always been beautiful.

Surviving

Even in your pain, I was here.
Even in your shame, I was here.
Even when you tried to run away, I was here.

I have never left; you just turned your back to me. But I have always been here speaking and moving. I have been here waiting. I have been here helping. I have been here because I'm not going anywhere.

I am here.

Kearsen Avendano

I love you so powerfully
And incredibly
So fully
And completely

I love you more than you'll ever know or think
More than you could even imagine

I love you
With all of me

Surviving

I'll say it once
And I'll say it again
As many times as you need
Until you believe
Everything you've ever dreamed
All of this
You will receive

Kearsen Avendano

You are not lost forever. This pain does not own you; it can no longer control you.

You are more. Don't let the lies cover the truth. Your value is priceless, more precious than every stone. Worthy of every happiness, every joy, every love. Even love to call your own.

You are strong, clothed in strength. To feel all that pain and get up once again. To heal, even though you could not see it then. To fight when you had no fight left. To hope when you only saw death.

You are beautiful as you are. Every flaw you think you have, even every scar. I know you may not see it or believe that you could be. But I see someone that is a masterpiece.

Intricate, wonderful, and unique.
One of a kind.

You are what I see.

Surviving

There is so much more for you
Don't give up
When the night is at its darkest
Is when the light shines the brightest

Kearsen Avendano

You are not alone. I know it feels like it at times. I know the weight of the world seems to build on your shoulders, drowning your mind. Give it to me, every pain and every fear. Give me your tears. Let me remove the weight so that you can see, so that you can hear. Then listen to my voice when I say,

I am here.

Surviving

You will not be abandoned
You will not be forgotten
My love for you will endure
Through the coldest winters
And past the furthest horizons

Kearsen Avendano

My arms carry the comfort your body aches for.
My eyes see you for who you truly are.
My voice is the peace you reach for.
My hands will take your every scar.
My heart is the love you search for.
My light will find you,
No matter how far.

Surviving

I will protect you as you walk along this path, shielding you with my body, fighting against every arrow and enemy. You will be untouched, unharmed by every hand.

Hidden in my arms,
In my love,
In my heart.

Whether by yourself or with my own, your feet will always stand.

Kearsen Avendano

You will be free
No more tape or glue
From the bottom of your feet
To everything you knew

Take a breath
Let it out
Take that step
Take that route

Surviving

    You are seen.
    You are heard.
    You are loved.
    You are more,

Than every thing you've been told
And every thing you've felt before.

    You are brave.
    You are valued.
    You are enough.
    You are needed.

And as you step out of the dark
Every pain will be defeated.

    You are accepted.
    You are worthy.
    You are beautiful.
    You are strong,

As you are and as you'll be.
You will always belong.

Kearsen Avendano

Breathe
Focus on my voice
Let it bring you peace
Let it calm the noise
I will bring all you need
Every shelter
Every safety
I will always be with you
I will help you break free

Surviving

Bring your brokenness
Bring your mess
Bring your shame and your hurt
Bring your fear
Bring your doubt
Bring your pride and your heart

Whenever you feel weak
Bring it to me
Lay it down at my feet
Take my hand
And let me lead

Kearsen Avendano

You can make it through this hurt, lifting your body off the floor, drying your tears, and taking that breath. You can find something to hold onto. Reaching and taking my hand, hearing my voice, following my steps.

So here I am, reaching for you, waiting for you. Listening patiently to your every word, your every concern as I whisper my love. Telling you the truth, showing that no matter what you go through or where it takes you, I have always been here. I will always help you.

Surviving

I'll be with you, even if the waves rock the boat. Through every storm, you won't be alone. I am here for you; stop trying to hold it together and let go.

Kearsen Avendano

Give me your every burden
Set it upon my shoulders
Lay down all your pain
Till there isn't any that remains
Let every tear fall at my feet
Place your hands in mine
For every shackle
I will defeat

Surviving

And when you notice
The old washing away
Turning to ashes
Before your eyes
Don't fear
But instead remember
In the new
You will rise
Beautiful
And wise

Kearsen Avendano

Follow
    my
        steps.

                Follow
                      my
                          light.

                                Follow
                                    my
                                        voice.

I promise you will be alright.
You will find peace.
You will have joy.

Surviving

Sometimes, you need to escape to be able to hang on. Your mind drifts to what's to come, seeing every dream that lies within your heart and every need you hope to reach. Living inside that fantasy, one that helps you find the strength to keep fighting. So you can make it to that reality.

Sometimes, you just need to take it one day at a time. Unable to think of tomorrow while standing in what is today. Fighting for what is now, hoping for better, yet completely exhausted. Fingers only strong enough to grasp this day, this time.

Sometimes you can't hold on.
Completely torn apart and aching. Yet you're still able to be held, carried in my arms. Because at that point, I will hold on. I will hold on to you; I will hold on for you.

So, continue to dance in the visions of your future and take the day as it comes. Continue to lay yourself into my palms. Whatever you can and whatever you can't.

Whatever it is, just continue.

Kearsen Avendano

Burn the broken pieces
Let them go
If you want better
You must demolish the old
Say goodbye to what was before
To who you were then
Because no longer
Will you be in the pain

Instead

You'll be on the other side
Watching the flames
So brightly they'll shine
Breaking through the dark
Leaving only ashes behind
And in return
Beauty
Is what you'll find

Surviving

It's going to be okay,
You will overcome this.

-I promise

Kearsen Avendano

Whether you're in the depths of the sea
Or stranded in the desert
On the highest mountain
Or the lowest valley

I will drain the oceans and tread every barren land
I will climb to the sky and light up every basin

All the lies will fall away
Each wall will crumble in my wake
All of this
I will do for you

Day or night
Sun or rain
I will do
Whatever it takes

Surviving

The reason that things have gotten so much harder
Is because you are that much closer to escaping
To reaching the better

Kearsen Avendano

You are more than their words
Than their lies
You deserve better
Someone who will love you for every inch
For every part that you hold
Every piece of you that broke
And for each one that becomes whole
Inside and out
Someone that will remind you of their love
Someone that will stay
And if that is not them
Please don't wait

Surviving

I will travel the path with you
Simply take my hand
No matter how dark the road gets
Even if you cannot stand
Don't listen to the whispers
That nibble at your ears
I will restore it all to you
You do not need to fear

All that you've lost
All that's been stolen
I will give you more
All the time spent battling
It will all be restored
Better than before

Kearsen Avendano

You will make it

You will reach it

You will see it

You will live it

And when you get there, you'll become a light like the one that once helped you.

Surviving

I know you've been fighting for long
Battling everything that has come
I know the sword weighs heavy
On your body
On your arms
I see your mind hesitates
To lay it down and be done
But I promise you'll continue
To be safe
To be loved

Set it at my feet
Lay yourself down
With all the fight you've given
It's time for rest to be found
I will take up the sword
If you'd give me the reins
Then you can finally breathe
As I break every chain

Kearsen Avendano

Focus on the touch of skin, the warmth that lies therein.
We will take it one step at a time. Breathe slowly out,

Then in.

Trust me to guide you through the night. Believe in me;
let me fight this fight. Let me carry you and be your legs
as we grow closer to the light, as you step out of pain.

Surviving

Allow your fingers to ease
Knuckles relaxing
Fists dissolving
Body silencing

You've held on for so long
Skin torn and blistered
Keeping the pieces together
With nothing but bare hands
And a bleeding heart
Now it's time to take a breath
To let go

Let your body find rest
In peace you will dwell
Just stop holding on
And you'll see that you are held

Stop listening to those who say you are not given more than you can handle.

You are because you were never supposed to handle it alone. You have never been alone, and you never will be. So, lay it in my arms. We will handle it together, you and me.

Surviving

I am here every step of the way. Through the depths of the valleys, I will walk with you; I will carry you.

And when you reach the other side, when you can touch every prayer and every dream, I will be there waiting.

I am here for you through everything.

Kearsen Avendano

I hear your every word,
But do you hear mine?

Do you hear my promises of a better life?
Do you feel my comfort for every cry?
Do you see my light shining upon you in the night?
Do you see me taking up this fight?
Do you know that for you, I will always provide?

Surviving

I am not far from you
I am not too busy
I am with you
In the midst of your suffering
I am by your side
Feeling every cry
And catching every tear
Giving you all my comfort
All my love
I am here

Kearsen Avendano

What is peace
And what could it truly be
If you were to give it a chance
I'm sure you would see
It's not a fantasy
Or simply a dream
It's a reality
For you and me
A place where we
Can be free

Surviving

Look at me. Look into my eyes. Feel my hands. I am here with you. I am here for you. You are not alone. You have me to stand with you, to fight every battle. I will be your shield, throwing myself in front of any trouble. I will be the sword against every pain, tearing down each enemy coming against your name. Let me be your comfort, holding you in my arms. I will wrap you in my embrace, keeping you safe from the dark.

Kearsen Avendano

Have you ever thought the reason you only see one set of footprints is not because you are alone but because I am carrying you?

Surviving

Get ready to believe
To see all that lies ahead
Get ready to receive
Every word I've ever said
Get ready to reach
All the dreams you've ever had

Get ready
To break out of this pit
Out of this pain
Removing all the sadness
And all the shame

You'll finally be in a place
Where nothing will ever be the same
You'll finally see the worth
That's on your name

Kearsen Avendano

When you're tired, exhausted, brought to the ground,
Remember that you are loved still.
When you have doubt, fear, and stress that cloud,
Remember that you are loved still.
When you feel broken, shattered, with nothing left,
Remember that you are loved still.
When it feels that you can't go on or catch your breath,
Remember that you are loved still.

Your pain will not last forever; it will soon end. And through it all, my love will stand.

Surviving

When you make it out
Because I know you will
You'll see the truth
And everything that's awaited you
You'll have finally reached
A life that's more
A life that's new

Kearsen Avendano

When you can't hope anymore
When you can't see anymore
When your soul is broken
And your heart lies beaten on the floor
When you can't trust anything
Not even yourself
When you have nothing left but a shell

Believe
Believe in my words
Believe in my hands
Believe in my love
Believe in my promises

Surviving

Even when you can't see it
Have faith and believe
Even when it doesn't make sense
Let me lead
I have told you
Of these hopes and dreams
And I've promised you a life
Filled with love and dignity
Know that through your days
My word is true
I will bring it to reality
And deliver you

Kearsen Avendano

You become a masterpiece after being made new through the pain that caused you to fall to pieces. It's when you reach the other side. When you're able to heal. When you can look back on the past without becoming lost in it.

And….

you've already started.

Surviving

You will be okay
No matter what tries to come against
I will make sure of it

So lift your head
And take my hand
Set down every broken piece
And take a stand

Against the hurt
Sorrow
And pain
Against the loneliness
Agony
And chains

Open your eyes
And look beyond
At the beauty that lies
On the brighter side
Of this valley you walk

Take that step
To believe and receive
All that you've waited for
The change that you hoped for
You'll hold it in your hands
And finally have a chance

Kearsen Avendano

Because nowhere else
Will you ever find
This kind of love
Or peace of mind

No where else
Will you actually be
Newly made
And fully free

Surviving

I'm giving myself to you
My heart
My arms
My hope
And strength

I'm giving my love to you
My healing
My peace
My forgiveness
And grace

I'm giving my all to you
My path
My rest
My light
And faith

I will be your shelter and your safe place

Kearsen Avendano

I reach my hand to you, waiting for your touch. Waiting for your faith in the more. To see you take that next step, the one that leads you closer to freedom. Closer to the light.

Keep your eyes on me, open your eyes to me. Allow yourself to feel my comfort, to feel my arms holding you through this. I'm right here with you, as you come out of the dark.

Every dream that helped you escape before, now awaiting you, right through this door. Have hope, believe. Take that breath and reach.

Surviving

In your hurt
In your pain
When all you felt was shame

In the now
In the new
In all that you do

You are loved
You are enough
This has always been true

Kearsen Avendano

The question isn't whether I'll do it for you,
It's whether you'll trust me to.
So, do you?

Surviving

Did you survive all the pain?
Barely.
And what will you do now?

Learn to not just survive, but to live.

Thank you for your patience, effort, vulnerability, and strength to make it through this book. I pray you have found something to hold onto as you escape your valley, that you have found some small piece of hope, of faith, a mustard seed worth. Because faith truly does move mountains.

If you have but a mustard seed worth of faith, nothing shall be impossible for you.
Matthew 17:20

Biblical Affirmations

God comforts you in all your troubles.
2 Corinthians 1:3-4

You are not alone; He is with you through the darkest nights and valleys.
Psalm 23:4

God hears your voice.
Psalm 116:1-2

You are forever loved.
Ephesians 2:4

Your troubles will soon be gone.
2 Corinthians 4:18

His promises for you are true.
Isaiah 55:11

God will never abandon you; He will save you.
Psalm 34:18

You will find healing in Him.
Psalm 147:3

God will give you a new strength and guide you.
Psalm 23:3

You were once darkness, but now you are light from the Lord.
Ephesians 5:8

He gives you peace unlike any other.
John 14:27

God draws you to Him.
John 6:44

You will find shelter and rest in Him.
Psalm 91:1

You are worth more than any ruby.
Proverbs 31:10

God is your shelter and safe place.
Psalm 9:9

You are fearfully and wonderfully made by Him.
Psalm 139:14

You are God's masterpiece.
Ephesians 2:10

About the Author

Kearsen Avendano is a poet, author, and mental health advocate who believes that healing is believing. She writes about mental health, hope, strength, faith, and more.

Her debut poetry collection, *Surviving*, was released in August 2023. This collection focuses on helping you find strength and light to make it through pain and darkness. She wrote this book to provide others with the words and strength she needed when going through her darkness.

Her second poetry collection, Finding You, was released on December 31, 2023. She wrote this collection from her perspective of how she came to reach healing, to help you overcome the pain left after making it out of the valley and to help you find healing as well.

When she's not writing, she is fishing with her family, working on her to be read list, or having conversations with someone about faith.

Kearsen pens a monthly newsletter about books and everything else. You can learn more at Kearsenavendano.com or by heading to @kearsenavendano on Instagram and Kearsen Avendano Poetry on Facebook.

Made in the USA
Middletown, DE
28 July 2024